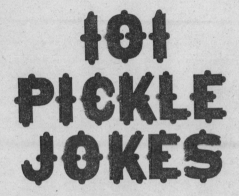

101 PICKLE JOKES

by
BOB VLASIC

Illustrated by Don Orehek

PYRAMID BOOKS   **NEW YORK**

101 PICKLE JOKES

A PYRAMID BOOK

Pyramid edition published August, 1974.

ISBN 0-515-03553-X
Library of Congress Catalog Card Number: 74-5976
Printed in the United States of America

Pyramid Books are published by Pyramid Communications, Inc. Its trademarks, consisting of the word "Pyramid" and the portrayal of a pyramid, are registered in the United States Patent Office.

Pyramid Communications, Inc., 919 Third Avenue, New York, N.Y. 10022

ABOUT THE AUTHOR

Bob Vlasic, author of 101 Pickle Jokes, has been "in a pickle"—so to speak— for 15 years. That is how long he has been in the pickle business. As America's largest retailer of pickles, Bob Vlasic knows everything there is to know about pickles—including the best pickle jokes (which he collects)... His book is a pickle barrel of laughs!

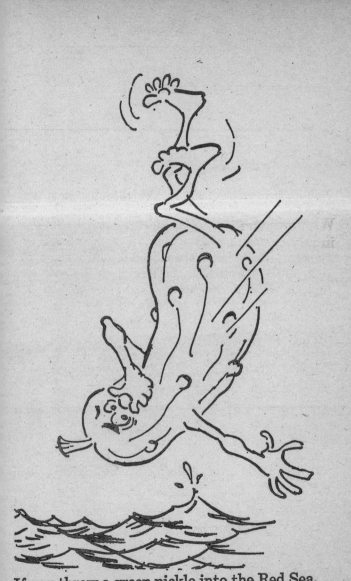

If you throw a green pickle into the Red Sea, what will it become?

Wet!

What's long, green, has holes, and you blow in it?

A Pickle-o!

What symbol appears in every Russian delicatessen?

A hammer and pickle.

What's the all-time hit musical play for pickles?

"Hello Dilly."

"Hey, Tom, you've got a pickle in your ear."
"What'd you say?"
"I SAID YOU'VE GOT—"
"You'll have to speak louder—I've got a pickle in my ear."

Why did the pickle climb the ladder to the roof?

He heard the meal was on the house!

If 10 pickles are a bunch and 20 pickles are a barrel, how much are 30 and 40?

Seventy!

What's every pickle's favorite game show?

Let's Make a Dill.

How can you tell which pickles are left-handed?

Place a giant bowl of pickles in front of someone, ask him to eat as many as he can, and the remaining pickles are left!

Who was known as the "man in the green flannel suit?"

Gregory Pickle.

What made the pickle break up with his fiance?

He soured on her.

2 3 4

1   5

20

19

18

17

Connect the dots, color it green, and what
have you got?

Writer's cramp!

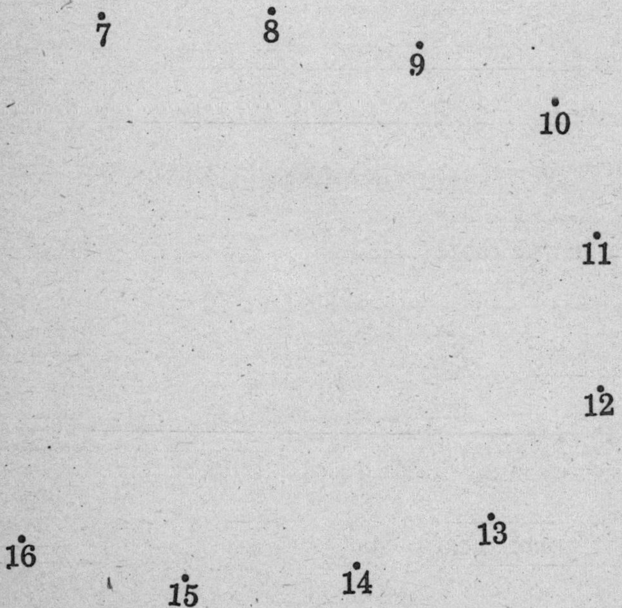

7

8

9

10

11

12

13

16

15

14

What do you call a sale on dill pickles?

A devaluation of the diller.

Who does the boy cucumber dig the most?

The pickle dish!

How do cucumbers go on strike?

They form pickle lines.

Who said, "I never met a pickle I didn't like"?

Dill Rogers!

How does a pickle learn?

He uses his brine!

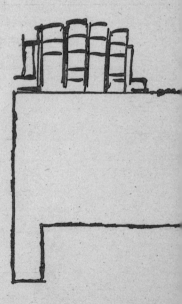

Why did the pickle close its eyes?

It saw the salad dressing.

What does every little gherkin dream of?

A house in the country with a white pickle fence!

Who is the pickles' favorite football player?

George Sauer!

Why are sour pickles so tasty?

Because they're dill-icious!

What's green and goes oink oink?

Porky Pickle!

What is green, is faster than a speeding bullet, more powerful than a locomotive, able to leap tall buildings at a single bound?

Super-pickle.

What is green and gets chased by dogs?

A pickle puss.

"Ralph, I think we have to fire our new cook."

"Why, dear?"

"She's so slow. This morning I asked her to dice some pickles, and she still isn't finished."

"Do you know why she's taking so long?"

"Yes, she's drawing black dots on them."

How do we know pickles are extremely jealous?

They turn green with envy!

Where do you usually find pickles?

The same place you left them.

Why does a pickle cross the road?

To get to the other side dish!

Will the real cute-cumber please stand up?

What kind of books do pickles like?

Spicy ones.

Why did the cucumber change color?

It was pickled pink!

CUSTOMER: How much are your pickles?
STOREKEEPER: Two for 15 cents.
CUSTOMER: How much is just one?
STOREKEEPER: Eight cents.
CUSTOMER: Okay, I'll take the other one.

What did one cucumber say to the other?

Boy, are we going to be pickled.

Who is the all-time favorite pickle gangster?

John Dill-inger!

Why doesn't a pickle like to travel?

Because it's a jarring experience.

If you ate five pickles and then ate three more, what would you have?

You'd have eight, and ate, and ate!

Why are pickles in sandwiches so polite?

They're well bread!

What do you call a dill that keeps changing color?

A fickle-pickle!

To what does a gherkin owe his good fortune?

The pickle finger of fate.

MAN: Miss Jones, why is there a pickle behind your ear?

MISS JONES: *Oh dear, I must have eaten my pencil for lunch.*

Why is it simple to condense pickle stories?

Because pickles are easy to digest.

What's green and shoots below par golf?

Jack Picklaus!

Pickle: "I'm not too well, Doctor. I keep thinking I'm a Great Dane."
Psychiatrist: "How long have you been feeling this way?"
Pickle: "Ever since I was a puppy."

What's green and goes slam, slam, slam, slam.

A four-door pickle!

What's green and writes underwater?

A ball-point pickle!

What's green and green and green and green and green ...

A pickle rolling downhill!

What is green and insulting?

Don Pickles.

What's the first line of the pickle wedding ceremony?

Dilly Beloved, we are gathered together...

Why do pickles go with sandwiches?

Because they're social climbers.

What's white on the outside and green on the inside?

A pickle sandwich.

Why do pickles have wrinkles?

They worry a lot.

What's the all-time hit song for pickles?

"He's Just My Dill."

What's green and swims in the sea?

Moby Pickle.

How do you make a pickle float?

Two scoops of ice cream, some soda and a large pickle!

How do you prepare a pickle sundae?

You start getting it ready Fridae and Satur-dae!

What do you call a girl who looks like a pickle?

A real live dill!

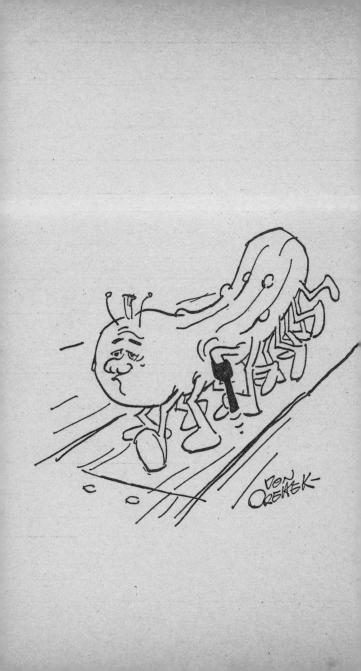

What is green and goes 99 thump, 99 thump, 99 thump.

A centipickle with a wooden leg.

What's the best way to call the pickle monster?

Long distance!

How many sides does a pickle have?

Two, an inside and an outside.

What do they call Martian gourmets?

Purple pickle-eaters!

Where do little pickles come from?

Inside the jar.

Did Emily Post say it is proper to eat pickles with the fingers?

No, she says pickles should be eaten separately.

How can you change a pickle into another vegetable?

You toss it in the air and it comes down squash!

What do you call bobbing for pickles?

A barrel of fun.

What happens when a pickle is bored?

He becomes very dill.

How do you spell pickle backwards?

P-i-c-k-l-e b-a-c-k-w-a-r-d-s.

Doctor, examining his patient: "My heavens, you must be upset. There's a cucumber growing out of your head."

Patient: *"Of course I'm upset. I planted corn."*

How do you pack 1,000 pickles into a small barrel?

Very carefully!

What do you do when a man with a shotgun demands all your pickles?

You give him both barrels!

What business does a smart pickle go into?

He opens a dilly-catessen!

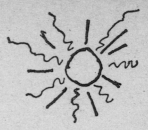

What's red and green?

A sunburned pickle!

Who was that pickle-o I saw you with last night?

That was no pickle-o, that was my fife!

How can you tell when there's 1,000 pounds of pickles under your bed?

You're closer to the ceiling.

What do you do to prevent bumps on a pickle?

Cover it with a mosquito net.

What's green and pecks on trees?

Woody Woodpickle!

Why do gherkins giggle a lot?

They're picklish.

Who's the toughest pickle in Dodge City?

Marshal Dill.

What's a shy pickle on his first date?

A little green around the girls!

Can you eat pickles with fingers?

No, pickles don't have fingers.

Why are pickles wary about lending money?

They're tired of people putting the bite on them.

How do you say pickle in French?

Pickle in French!

Should you ever eat pickles on an empty stomach?

No, always use a plate instead!

Why didn't the pickle cross the sandwich?

To keep from coming through the rye.

What gives a pickle good taste?

Four years in an Ivy League school.

What's the phrase heard most often at pickle card games?

Dill me in.

What's the difference between a dime pickle and a quarter pickle?

Fifteen cents!

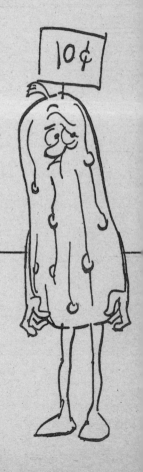

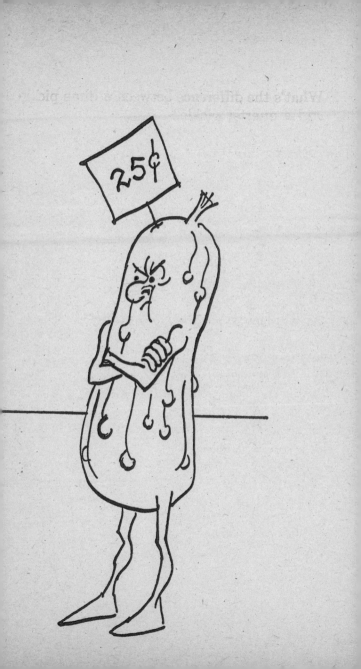

Why did the pickle wear red suspenders?

The blue ones broke!

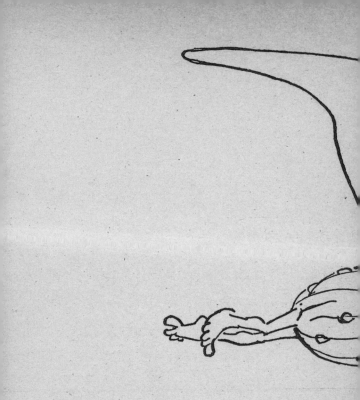

What's green and soars through the air?

Jonathan Livingston Pickle.

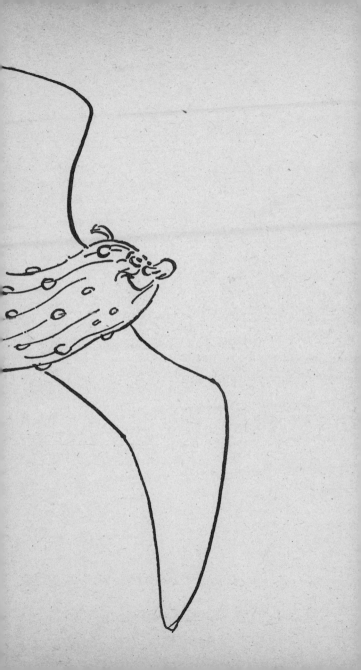

Who is the pickle Knute Rockne?

Pat O'Brine.

What is long, green, noisy and very dangerous?

A thundering herd of pickles!

When a cucumber tours England, where does it go first?

Pickledilly Circus.

What's green and white, green and white, green and white, etc.?

A pickle rolling down a snowbank!

How do you make a pickle sour?

The same way you make a whiskey sour— only use a pickle!

Why did the pickle take a ladder to school?

It was going to high school.

What's a pickle's favorite TV show?

"What's My Brine."

What do you do with a pickle when it's a year old?

Wish it a happy birthday.

What's green, then yellow, then green, then yellow, then green, then yellow?

A pickle that moonlights as a banana.

What famous Hollywood producer has a cellar full of pickles?

Barrel Zanuck!

Knock, knock.
Who's there?
Pickle.
Pickle who?
Pickle letter from A to Z.

How do you make a pickle laugh?

Tell it an elephant joke.

IQ Test: A pickle worker was five feet tall and wore a size eight shoe. What did he weigh?

Pickles, of course!

How does a pickle eat when he's hungry?

With relish.

Name a Hollywood producer?

Mike Pickles!

BEAUTY CONTEST

Which pickle wins the beauty contest?

The pickle of the crop!

What's green, has 22 legs and plays football in cold weather?

The Green Bay Pickles.

Some good news and some bad news. First the bad news. A monster pickle is attacking the city. Now the good news. Instead of eating you, you eat it.

What comes after pickle-N?

Pickle-O.

To remove a pickle from a jar, the jar must first be what?

Topless.

Where does a gherkin go skiing?

Pike's Pickle.

Who is the pickles' favorite comedian?

Green Skelton!

If you had 20 barrels of pickles in your kitchen and had 20 barrels of relish brought in, what would you have?

A very large kitchen.

How do you make a green pickle?

Cross a blue pickle with a yellow one!

How does a ghost eat a pickle?

By goblin it!

If corn has ears and potatoes have eyes,
what do pickles have?

Each other.